First World War
and Army of Occupation
War Diary
France, Belgium and Germany

14 DIVISION
43 Infantry Brigade
Suffolk Regiment
12th Battalion
1 June 1918 - 31 May 1919

WO95/1910/4

The Naval & Military Press Ltd
www.nmarchive.com
Published in association with The National Archives

Published by

The Naval & Military Press Ltd

Unit 10 Ridgewood Industrial Park,

Uckfield, East Sussex,

TN22 5QE England

Tel: +44 (0) 1825 749494

www.naval-military-press.com

www.nmarchive.com

This diary has been reprinted in facsimile from the original. Any imperfections are inevitably reproduced and the quality may fall short of modern type and cartographic standards.

© Crown Copyright
Images reproduced by permission of The National Archives, London, England, 2015.

Contents

Document type	Place/Title	Date From	Date To
Heading	WO95/1910/4 14 Div-43 Inf Bde 12 Suffolk Regt Jun 1918-May 1919		
Heading	12th Bn Suffolk Regt Jun 1918-May 1919 14th Division 43rd Infy Bde From To Div 121 Bde		
Heading	War Diary 12th Suffolk Regt June 1918 Vol 22		
War Diary	Nordpeene	01/06/1918	02/06/1918
War Diary	Noard peene	03/06/1918	03/06/1918
War Diary	Cassel	04/06/1918	15/06/1918
War Diary	Boulogne	16/06/1918	16/06/1918
War Diary	Pirbright	17/06/1918	30/06/1918
War Diary	War Diary. 12th Bn. Suffolk Regt. July 1918. Nov 1919 Vol 23		
War Diary	Pirbright	01/07/1918	03/07/1918
War Diary	Shornecliff	04/07/1918	04/07/1918
War Diary	Boulogne	05/07/1918	05/07/1918
War Diary	Boursin	06/07/1918	10/07/1918
War Diary	Licques	11/07/1918	11/07/1918
War Diary	Zouafques	12/07/1918	12/07/1918
War Diary	Bayenghem-Lez Eperlecques	13/07/1918	31/07/1918
Miscellaneous			
Heading	12th Bn The Suffolk Regt War Diary August 1918 Vol 24		
War Diary	Bayenghem Lez-Eperleques	01/08/1918	12/08/1918
War Diary	Lederzeele	13/08/1918	13/08/1918
War Diary	Bissezeele	14/08/1918	14/08/1918
War Diary	Droglandt.	15/08/1918	16/08/1918
War Diary	Proven	17/08/1918	17/08/1918
War Diary	Brake Camp Hagle. N. Of Vlamertinghe	18/08/1918	18/08/1918
War Diary	Support Line.	19/08/1918	22/08/1918
War Diary	Frontline	23/08/1918	27/08/1918
War Diary	Reserve Orilla Camp N.W. Of Vlamertinghe.	28/08/1918	31/08/1918
Miscellaneous			
Heading	War Diary. 12th Bn Suffolk Regt September 1918 Vol 28		
War Diary	Supportline Ypers Sector	31/08/1918	05/09/1918
War Diary	Frontline Ypres Sector.	06/09/1918	10/09/1918
War Diary	Riserve Camp N.W. Of Vlamertinghe	11/09/1918	13/09/1918
War Diary	Janter Biezen	14/09/1918	19/09/1918
War Diary	St-Laurent	20/09/1918	24/09/1918
War Diary	Frontline	25/09/1918	27/09/1918
War Diary	Bluff-Canal Sector	28/09/1918	29/09/1918
War Diary	Dickebusch.	29/09/1918	30/09/1918
Miscellaneous	12th Battalion The Suffolk Regiment.		
Miscellaneous	14th Division. Report On Operations. 28th September. 1918	28/09/1918	28/09/1918
Miscellaneous	Operation Order By Lieut Colonel. L. Lloyd. D.S.O. Bn The Suffolk Regiment.	27/09/1918	27/09/1918
Miscellaneous			
Heading	War Diary 12th Suffolk Regt October 1918 Vol 29		
War Diary	Dickebush Ypres-Potijle Road.	01/10/1918	11/10/1918

War Diary	Wulvergem	12/10/1918	14/10/1918
War Diary	Front Line at Wervicq on River Lys	15/10/1918	15/10/1918
War Diary	Active Operations	16/10/1918	20/10/1918
War Diary	Evregnies	21/10/1918	31/10/1918
Heading	War Diary 12th Suffolk Regt November 1918 Vol 30		
War Diary	Evregnies	01/11/1918	07/11/1918
War Diary	Front Line Espierre Sector	08/11/1918	10/11/1918
War Diary	List of Molembaix.	11/11/1918	12/11/1918
War Diary	Evregnies	13/11/1918	14/11/1918
War Diary	Turcoing	15/11/1918	30/11/1918
Miscellaneous			
Heading	War Diary 12th Suffolk Regt December 1918 Vol 31		
War Diary	Tourcoing	01/12/1918	31/12/1918
Miscellaneous	12th Battalion The Suffolk Regiment.		
Heading	War Diary 12th Suffolk Regt January 1919 Vol 32		
War Diary		04/01/1919	31/01/1919
War Diary	Bondues	01/02/1919	28/02/1919
Miscellaneous	12th Bn. The Suffolk Regiment	01/02/1919	01/02/1919
Heading	War Diary 12th Bn Suffolk Regt March 1919 Vol 34		
War Diary	Bondues Nr Lille.	01/03/1919	31/03/1919
Miscellaneous	12th Bn The Suffolk Regt.		
War Diary	Bondues.	01/04/1919	02/04/1919
War Diary	Herseaux	03/04/1919	30/04/1919
Miscellaneous	12th Bn Suffolk Regt.		
War Diary	Herseaux. (Petit Aupenarde)	01/05/1919	31/05/1919
Miscellaneous	12th Bn Suffolk Regt.	31/05/1919	31/05/1919

MDGS/1910-24

14 Div - 43 Inf Bde

Dominion 12 Suffolks Rest

Jun 1918 - May 1919

12TH BN SUFFOLK REGT
JUN ~~JLY~~ 1918-MAY 1919

14TH DIVISION
43RD INFY BDE

From to DIV   12/BDE

$\frac{43}{14}$

War Diary

12th Suffolk Regt

June 1918

12th Bn Suffolk Regt. WAR DIARY or INTELLIGENCE SUMMARY. June 1918. Army Form C. 2118.

(Erase heading not required)

Place	Date	Hour	Summary of Events and Information	Remarks and references to Appendices
NORDPEENE	1st & 2nd		In camp. hd	
NORDPEENE	3rd		Moved by march route to camp at a chateau S.E. of CASSEL. hd	
CASSEL	4th – 15th		In camp – preparing scheme for defending given area. hd	
BOULOGNE	16th		By train to BOULOGNE – night in rest camp. hd	
PIRBRIGHT	17th		Cross Channel to FOLKESTONE thence by train to BROOKWOOD, SURREY to camp at hd	
			STONYCASTLE.	
PIRBRIGHT	18th		Marched to BULLSWATER CAMP, PIRBRIGHT. hd	
"	19th		Drafts numbering 674 from various units arrived to form Battalion, all B II	
			category. hd	
"	25 – 30th		Training reorganizing into Battalion. hd	

M Mun
Captain
O/C 12th Bn Suffolk Regt.

WAR DIARY.

12th Bn. Suffolk Regt.

July 1918.

Army Form C. 2118.

12th Bn Suffolk Regt WAR DIARY or INTELLIGENCE SUMMARY.

July 1918.

(Erase heading not required.)

Instructions regarding War Diaries and Intelligence Summaries are contained in F.S. Regs., Part II. and the Staff Manual respectively. Title pages will be prepared in manuscript.

Place	Date JULY	Hour	Summary of Events and Information	Remarks and references to Appendices
PIRBRIGHT	1st–3rd		In Camp Training & organising. AW.	
SHORNECLIFF	4th		By Train to No 1 Camp SHORNECLIFF. AW.	
BOULOGNE	5th		Cross Channel in morning - Encamped night No 5 Rest Camp BOULOGNE. AW.	
BOURSIN	6th		Entrained BOULOGNE to MARQUISE - thence by route march to Buiés in BOURSIN AW.	
BOURSIN	6th–10th		TRAINING. AW.	
LICQUES	11th		Marched to Buiés à LICQUES. AW.	
ZOUAFQUES	12th		Marched to Buiés à ZOUAFQUES. AW.	
BAYENGHEM-LEZ-EPERLECQUES	13th		Marched to Buiés à BAYENGHEM-LEZ-EPERLECQUES. AW.	
BAYENGHEM-LEZ-EPERLECQUES	14th–31st		Training in area of BAYENGHEM-LEZ-EPERLECQUES. AW.	

[signature]
CAPT. & ADJT.
12th BATT. SUFFOLK REGT.

	OFFICERS	OTHER RANKS
STRENGTH for 1st JULY. 1918.	41	592
STRENGTH for 31st JULY 1918.	42	834
CASUALTIES during MONTH :-		NIL
REINFORCEMENTS during MONTH :-	1	293
AWARDS during MONTH :-		NIL

OFFICERS - REINFORCEMENTS :-
   CAPTAIN. H. LEEMING   JOINED for DUTY   10-7-18.
                                      DESPATCHED 1/4th SUFFOLKS. 18-7-18.
                                      REJOINED for DUTY   29-7-18

12th Bn. The Suffolk Regt.

War Diary.

AUGUST 1918

12th Bn Suffolk Regt

WAR DIARY
or
INTELLIGENCE SUMMARY

Army Form C. 2118.

August 1918

Place	Date	Hour	Summary of Events and Information	Remarks and references to Appendices
BAYENGHEM-LEZ-EPERLECQUES	1st-12th		Training in BAYENGHEM.	
LEDERZEELE	13th		Marched to LEDERZEELE.	
BISSEZEELE	14th		" " BISSEZEELE.	
DROGLANDT	15th		" " DROGLANDT.	
"	16th		Billets at DROGLANDT.	
PROVEN	17th		Marched to PROVEN.	
BRAKE CAMP	18th		Moved by light railway to Camp at HAGLE.	
HAGLE N. of VLAMERTINGHE				
SUPPORT LINE	19th-22nd		Marched to support positions of right Bde sector of YPRES sector. Relieved 1/5th K.O.Y.L.I. 49th Division. Relieving 205 Middlesex Regt in front line of right Bde sector.	
FRONT LINE	23rd-28th			
Reserve in ORILLA Camp N. of VLAMERTINGHE	28th	3p.	In Bde Reserve in ORILLA camp N.W. of VLAMERTINGHE.	

A. N. [signature]
CAPT. & ADJT.
12th BATT. SUFFOLK REGT.

	OFF	O.R.
STRENGTH for 1st August 1918	42	838
STRENGTH for 31st August 1918	42	905
CASUALTIES during MONTH		3
REINFORCEMENTS during MONTH.		93
AWARDS during MONTH.		NIL.

signature
CAPT. & ADJT.
11th BATT. SUFFOLK REGT.

War Diary

12th Bn Suffolk Regt

September 1918

12th Bn Suffolk Regt

WAR DIARY or **INTELLIGENCE SUMMARY**

Army Form C. 2118

September 1918

Place	Date	Hour	Summary of Events and Information	Remarks and references to Appendices
SUPPORT LINE YPRES SECTOR	31st Aug	1.30p	Bn relieved the 8/Bn Hx in Support line West of YPRES.	W
"	1st Sept	1 – 5th	Bn in Support line YPRES sector.	
Front line YPRES Sector	6th – 7th		Bn relieved the 20th Mx in front line. YPRES Sector.	W
"	7th – 10th		Bn in front line YPRES sector.	W
Reserve camp	11th		Bn relieved further hrs by 10th H.L.I. + came into reserve at O'RIEN camp	W
M.S. of VLAMERTINGHE	11/12th		Bn in reserve at O'RIEN camp.	
"	12 – 13th		Bn in reserve by light railway K School camp, ST JAN-TER-BIEZEN (W. of POPERINGHE)	W
TAN-TER BIEZEN	14th		Bn moved by light railway K School camp, ST JAN-TER-BIEZEN	W
"	14 – 19		Training in camp of School camp ST JAN-TER BIEZEN	W
ST LAURENT	20th		Bn marched two by companies at ST LAURENT (N. of STEENVOORDE)	W
"	20th – 24th		Bn in reserves at ST LAURENT	W
Front line	25th – 27th		Bn in front line in CANAL SECTOR N.E of VORMEZEELE	W
Buff - Canal Sector	28/29th		Active operation – narrative reports attached	W
DICKEBUSH	29 & 30th		Bn withdrew from action + marched to camp at DICKEBUSH	W

12th Battalion The Suffolk Regiment.

	Officers.	Other Ranks.
Strength first of month (September).	41.	879.
" Last " " (4th Oct.)	38.	758.
Reinforcements.	-	18.

Casualties during the month.

    2/Lieutenant F.J. DOUSS, M.C.
    2/Lieutenant W.T. CARLISLE.
    2/Lieutenant A.M. CHEQUER.

    Other Ranks 119.

[signed] Captain Adjt.
12th Suffolks.

SECRET.   43rd Brigade G.S. 669.

14th Division.

REPORT ON OPERATIONS.   28th SEPTEMBER, 1918.

1. **Strength of Brigade** (troops which actually took part in the attack)

3 Battalions.	12th Suffolk Regt.	20 Officers	556 O.Rs.)	Off.	O.Rs.
	20th Midx.Regt.	16 "	545 ")		
	10th H.L.I.	21 "	445 ")	57	1546.

   2 Sections 43rd Trench Mortar Battery.   2   26.
   3 Sections "A" Coy. 14th Machine Gun Battalion.   3   74.
   ½ Section 184th Tunnelling Company R.E.   1   21.
                                        Grand Total.   63   1667

2. **Dispositions.**

   The attack was carried out by the 20th Middlesex Regt. on the Right, the 12th Suffolk Regt. on the left, with the 10th H.L.I. in Brigade Reserve.
   The 42nd Infantry Brigade attacked on our Right and the 105th Infantry Brigade (35th Division) on our Left.

3. **Boundaries.**

   (a) Northern Boundary : 28/H.28.a.5.8. - 29.b.1.8. - Northern outskirts of CAFE FARM grounds - H.30.b.1.3. - I25. c.1.8. - 33.b.1.9. - 34.a.2.4. - d.15.65. - 0.5.a.7.0.

   (b) Southern boundary : 28/H.28.c.6.6. - Southern outskirts of ENGLISH WOOD - N.E. outskirts of MIDDLESEX WOOD - thence along light railway to I.32.a.0.1. - I.32.d.35.40. - 0.3.d.00.65. 4.c.4.0.

   (c) The YPRES-COMINES CANAL formed the boundary between the two leading Battalions.

4. **Attack formation.**
   Each leading Battalion attacked with two companies in front and two in support, the attacking waves being in lines of "worms" (section columns in single file).

5. **Assembly.**
   Front companies formed up for the attack along MIDDLESEX ROAD. Support companies formed up 400 yards in rear, along a tape on the right and along a light railway on the left.
   No one was allowed to cross MIDDLESEX ROAD during the assembly,
/more as troops on the road would have been visible to the enemy than in the dark ground in rear.
   The assembly was carried out without noise or interference from the enemy, all helmets, brasses and bayonets having been dulled.
   The move was completed one hour before zero.

6. **Features.**
The canal was a disadvantage, as it interfered with lateral communication between battalions.
The ground over which the attack was made rose gradually from MIDDLESEX ROAD and was deeply pitted with sheel holes and over grown with woods, with a certain amount of broken wire.
Along the Canal the SPOIL BANKS on wither side rose to about 20 or 30 feet but the top was covered with shell holes and the going was bad.
The most important feature was the BLUFF on the North Bank. Approaching it the ground sank into a hollow running across our front with a pond or patch of boggy ground 30 to 50 yards long at the foot of the BLUFF.
Beyond this the BLUFF rose up in a steep wall, some 50 to 70 feet high, approached on the Right by the SPOIL BANK, which narrowed to a yard or two in width and rose gradually in a neck which much pitted with sheel holes. The hollow ground rose up the left and the path way gave easy excess to the BLUFF on the left side of the pond, which was practically impassable. Beyond the South wall of the BLUFF ground descended steeply rising again over the S. Wall of A. CRATER.
The BLUFF bristled with M.G's and T.M's. and, if held with determination, should have proved an insurmountable obstacle.
Beyond the BLUFF the ground traversed was on a high level than the S. Bank of the CANAL, with some broken trenches, and ending in another rise to the Triangular BLUFF.
On the S. Side of the CANAL the ground rose gradually to the WHITE CHATEAU, which consists of a ruined mound and from which a fine view is obtained across the Northern slopes of the CANAL, and all the country to the E. of MENIN to WARNETON, and to the S. to the MESSINES RIDGE. Its possession by the enemy would have caused serious inconwenience to our troops holding the Mud Bank. Our hold on it was rendered secure by pushing platoons under the 55 metre conture and thus covering the ground to the S. while on the E. SPADGERS LANE, a sunken road, covered the front and stopped any chance of a counter-attack from the Germans massing in the dead ground to the S.E.
The occupation of the WHITE CHATEAU, therefore, enabled us to command the low ground between the two 55 metre plateaus, viz., the DAMM STRASSE to the S. and the one round HILL 60 to the N.

7. **The attack.**
Although battalions were very weak and the men belonged almost entirely to "B" Category, yet they were filled with keenness and confident of success. They moved across the ground with energy keeping close to the barrage. The chief incident was the capture of the BLUFF, "A" Company taking it in front and avoidig the front whilst "B" Company drwaing off all available men from its left wheeled round and encircled it on the left. Enemy showed some determination to hold it at first against the frontal attack, but when he perceived the encircling movement he lost heart and gave way.
I think the greatest praise is due to Captain LEEMING for his handling of the left company. He acted with the greatest promptness, coolness and skill, and his enveloping move was the great event of the day. If there had been any delay the enemy have probably taken heart and beaten off the frontal attack and then had time to deal with to belated front-attack- flank attack, but carried out promptly it took the enemy by surprise and the BLUFF was captured. The whole success of our advance hinged on this. If we had failed here no advance would have been made S. of the CANAL. The enemy could have counter-attacked and pushed us back along the whole Southern Front. The possession of the BLUFF made this ground secure and the position of the enemy on the MESSINES RIDGE was untenable.

At the same time the greatest credit to "A" Company which had the hardest task in making the frontal attack which was carried with such vigour that it kept the enemy fully occupied, whilst the flank attack was maturing.

In the second objective the 12th Suffolks had to make a complete wheel pivoting on their right through a system of trenches against the Triangular BLUFF which was situated at the apex of their second objective. This was carried out without much fighting.

8. I should like to draw special attention to the skill with which Lieut Col L.LLOYD. D.S.O. 12th Suffolk Regt. and Major W.W.MILNE M.C. Acting Commanding 20th Middlesex Regiment handled their Battalions; their instructions were very precise and thorough, and they were untiring in supervising. A half section of the 184th Tunnelling Company worked well. 14 known tunnels and dug-outs had to be cleared and at least four of these were found to have been mined, and were rendered harmless.

The Infantry were loud in their praise of the Artillery Barrage, which gave them the greatest confidence by its accuracy and volume.

9. The Huns generally put up a very poor fight and were entirely taken by complete surprise, though they claim to have been warned of the attack, everything showed that they were quite unready.

10. I think it would be a good thing if the contours could be more clearly marked on maps, or if a limited number of plain contoured maps with a few promising land marks could be made for the use of C.O's and Company Commanders. They would then more easily pick out the lie of the ground, note the dead ground and plan out their dispositions.

11. <u>Prisoners and material captured and enemy killed.</u>

	Estimated enemy killed.	Prisoners.	Guns.	T.M's.	M.G's.	Various.
12th Suffolks.	80 to 100.	150 to 200.	1.77. mm.	2.6".	12 or 13.	1 periscopic range finder 2 antie tank rifles. 1 Dressing station complete Rifles. Revolvers. Periscopes. Signalling gear.

(Signed) G. PERIERA. Brigadier General,
Commanding 43rd Infantry Brigade.

Certified true extracts from B.G. C'os narrative of operations. Extracted to form narrative of Bonapart in action 28th September

R.A. Lowe
Capt/Ady.
12 Suffolks

7/10/18.

OPERATION ORDER

BY

Lieut Colonel . L. Lloyd. D.S.O.
Bn The Suffolk Regiment.

In - The - Field.   27ᵀᴴ September

No. 1. The Battalion will carry out an attack at a time to be notified later.
The Battalion Middlesex Regiment will attack on our right and the Battalion N. STAFFORDS on our left at the same time.

No. 2. Our objectives are as follows :-
1st Objective. Line running from Point on CANAL at O.4.a.35.87. N.E. to I.34.d.2.5.
2nd Objective. Line of N. Bank of CANAL from O.4.a.35.87 to O.5.a.2.2. - (see maps already marked)

No. 3. Boundaries.
Battalion Right Boundary:— North BANK of CANAL.
Battalion LEFT Boundary:— Line running from point on Middlesex Road at I.33.B.05.85.-COME inclusive - I.34.D.15.63 to O.5.A.2.2.
Inter Company Boundary:— Line running from Middlesex Road I.33.A.71.67. to point of re-entrant T.34.C.50.62.

No. 4. Dispositions

"A" Company. Right front Line.
"B" Company. Left front Line.
"C" Company. Right Support.
"D" Company. Left Support.
B.H.Qrs.   I.32.A.90.99.
1 Section T.M.B. attached right front Company.

No. 5. Assembly Positions.
(a). Front Line Companies will assemble in 2 waves of "Worms". First wave on line immediately west of Middlesex Road from N. Bank of CANAL to I.33.B.05.85.
Second wave in "Worms" 50x yards in rear of 1st wave.
(b). Support Companies in two waves of "Worms" at same interval along the line of Light Railway from I.32.B.30.45 N.E. to I.26.D.93.03.
Companies will be in position at least 1 hour before ZERO, and will notify advance B.H.Q. when in position.

No. 6. Advance.

The Battalion will advance with "A" Company on CANAL BANK. "B" Company in touch with N. STAFFORDS – Left section "B" Company will overlap right Section N. STAFFORDS.

"A" Company will have RIGHT Platoon moving on top of SPOIL BANK and LEFT PLATOON below, each with 1 Platoon in Support.

Right Platoon will furnish a patrol to move along CANAL WALK – keeping time with general advance + to prevent a flank attack from CANAL.

"B" Company will advance with left section on line to COMAX inclusive and right Section keeping in touch with "A" Company.

O.C. "B" Company must be prepared to give every assistance to O.C. "A" Company to ensure capture of BLUFF – by envelopement – and will if necessary hold his left very lightly and throw every man he can spare against the BLUFF.

Support Companies will advance at same time as front Companies, and will be EAST of Light Railway line by Zero X 1 min, and not halt until about 50 yards EAST of Middlesex Road.

O.C. "C" Company will be prepared to furnish immediately reinforcements to O.C. "A" Company upon his request.

All reinforcements will come under orders of front line Commanders + Support.

Company Commanders will inform B.H.Q. immediately they have supplied reinforcements.

When first objective has been captured Companies will consolidate during the time allotted i.e. 63 mins.

Patrols will not be pushed forward on securing 1st objective, as a Rolling barrage will be put down.

B.H.Q. will be advised by all Companies immediately first objective is captured, and upon receipt of this information will move forward to I 33. D. 4. 6.

During Consolidation of first objective Light Trench mortars will bombard the Quadrilateral trenches running from I. 34. D. to O. 4. 6.

The left Company must be prepared to take any Counter attack in flank, arising from above trenches.

No. 7. Final Objective.

At ZERO plus 100. Companies will continue to advance to final objective, the left Company swinging to the right and conforming to the line of CANAL BANK.

Capture of final objective to be reported at once to Battalion H. Qrs.

The Battalion will then be in Support to Middlesex Regiment. Companies will reorganize at final position in depth.

In the event of gaps occuring between front Companies O.C. Support Companies must be prepared to cover gap especially with Lewis Gun fire.

No Special Light Signals, except those laid down for the S.O.S will be used during the operations.

No. 8. Method of Advance under Barrage.

The Barrage will open at ZERO minus five mins, and will lift off starting line at ZERO hour.

The Battalion will advance at ZERO hour as follows:—

```
     1st 100 yards   3 mins  =  ZERO +  3
     2nd   "    "    3   "   =    "  +  6
     3rd   "    "    3   "   =    "  +  9
     4th   "    "    3   "   =    "  + 12
*    5th   "    "    6   "   =    "  + 18
     6th   "    "    3   "   =    "  + 21
     7th   "    "    3   "   =    "  + 24
     8th   "    "    3   "   =    "  + 27
     9th   "    "    3   "   =    "  + 30
*   10th   "    "    6   "   =    "  + 36
    11th   "    "    3   "   =    "  + 39.
```

First objectives reached.

Barrage will roll until ZERO + 96. when it will again drop in front of first objective for 4 mins.

At ZERO plus 100 barrage will lift as follows:—

```
     1st 100 yards  3 mins  =  ZERO + 103 mins
     2nd   "    "   3   "   =    "  + 106  "
     3rd   "    "   3   "   =    "  + 109  "
     4th   "    "   3   "   =    "  + 112  "
     5th   "    "   3   "   =    "  + 115  "
     6th   "    "   3   "   =    "  + 118  "
     7th   "    "   3   "   =    "  + 121  "
```

Final objective reached by Battalion barrage will remain Stationary for 8 mins in front of final objective i.e. till ZERO plus. 129.

No. 9. Aeroplane Co-operation.

(a). A Contact aeroplane with streamer on tail and a black flap on each lower plane, will fly along the front at the next clock hour, but one after ZERO and at every clock hour after. Leading Troops will signal their positions on demand with maps and discs.

(b) A Counter attack aeroplane will patrol front from ZERO plus 40 onwards, and will signal enemy counter attack by firing a red parachute flare.

No. 10. Prisoners of War will be sent to Battalion HQrs.

Wounded will only be sent to R.A.P. at Battalion H.Q. by Stretcher Bearers.

Compass bearing of attack 140 degrees magnetic from Middlesex Road. Officers will be responsible for keeping direction.

Each man will carry 170 Rounds of S.A.A. and full water bottle.

5. S.O.S. Grenades per Company will be carried.

No dug-out will be entered except by tunnelling party with escort until reported by Tunnellers to be free from contact mines. Dug-outs will be labelled either "EXAMINED" or "DANGEROUS" by Tunnellers.

Crew Vaughan
for Lieut Colonel Lieut
Bn Suffolk Regiment.

S'iaff.s

WAR DIARY

12th Suffolk Regt

October 1918

Diary 2nd Bn the Suffolk Regt   Sheet I.   Army Form C. 2118.

WAR DIARY
or
INTELLIGENCE SUMMARY.
(Erase heading not required.)

October 1918.

Instructions regarding War Diaries and Intelligence Summaries are contained in F. S. Regs., Part II. and the Staff Manual respectively. Title pages will be prepared in manuscript.

Place	Date	Hour	Summary of Events and Information	Remarks and references to Appendices
DICKEBUSH YPRES-POTIJZE ROAD.	1st	2.05	In camp. Marched to camp 2000 yards E of YPRES on ZONNEBEKE road, and commenced work remaking MENIN road at HOOGE.	
"	3rd/11th		In camp and Battalion working as above.	
WULVERGEM.	12th		By train to WULVERGEM.	
"	13th/14th		In camp at WULVERGEM.	
Front Line at WERVICQ on River LYS	15th		Marched to line and relieved 2/23rd London Regiment.	
Active Operations	16th		Battalion crossed LYS and advanced, and occupied high ground and valley in front of PAUL BUCQ.	
"	17th		Battalion advanced and occupied line west of RONCQ.	
"	18th		Battalion in support advanced and occupied support line 20th Middlesex and 10th H.L.I. in neighbourhood of RISQUON TOUS.	
"	19th		Battalion advanced and occupied line East of HERSEAUX – PETIT AUDENARDE and in afternoon passed through 31st Division and occupied a line East of QUEVAUX camp - EVREGNIES.	
"	20th		Battalion attacked and occupied line from ESPIERRE CANAL DOTTIGNIES as first objective and then crossing CANAL enemy on Right SCHELT occupying a line on West bank of SCHELT from WACOING to junction of CANAL L'ESPIERRE and river ECAULT South of ESPIERRE.	

Army Form C. 2118.

Duplicate. 12th Bn The Suffolk Regt. Sheet II

WAR DIARY
INTELLIGENCE SUMMARY
October 1918.

Place	Date	Hour	Summary of Events and Information	Remarks and references to Appendices
EVREGNIES	21st		Battalion returned in front line for 10th Argyle & Sutherland Highlanders and Brigade came into support. Battalion marched to Billets at EVREGNIES. Refitting and Battalion in billets. training.	
EVREGNIES	22nd		Battalion in billets — training	
EVREGNIES	22/31st			

Lewis Burnham
Major & Adjutant
for Lieut Colonel
Commanding 12th Batt. Suffolk Regiment

War Diary

12th Suffolk Regt

November 1918

November 1918 WAR DIARY 12th Bn. The Suffolk Regt. Army Form C. 2118.
or
INTELLIGENCE SUMMARY.
(Erase heading not required.)

Place	Date	Hour	Summary of Events and Information	Remarks and references to Appendices
EVREGNIES	7th		In billets. Training. A/d	
Front line ESPIERRE Sect.	8th		Bn relieved 18th Bn York & Lancs in front line in trench tracks of SPITAALT A/d	
	7/9th August		"B" Coy front party of river to MERVRE'S A/d	
	9th		Bn crossed river at WARCOING, T. advanced to line running N + S	
	10th		1500 yards west of MOLENBAIX A/d Division sprayed on by 29th Div [140th] Div. crossing our front + remained in billets in farms west of MOLENBAIX A/d	
bul of MOLENBAIX	11th		In billets. Hostilities ceased at 11 am A/d	
"	12th		" "	
EVREGNIES	13th 14th		In billets. Moved by motor write A/d	
TURCOING	15th		Thereby march route to billets in TURCOING.	
TURCOING	16th 30th		In billets. Ceremonial drill, competition, recreational training and educational classes A/d	

W. M. [signature]
Captain.

	Officers.	Other Ranks.
Strength first of month.	39.	735.
Strength last of month.	43.	793.
Casualties.	N I L.	
Reinforcements :-		28.

    2/Lieutenant R.E. Gooch.
      " C.H. Cockerton.
      " R.W. Cawse.
      " R.G. Hart-Davies.
      " R.G. Evans.
      " A.M. Murtrie.
      " P.A. Bourjeaurd.

Honours and Awards :-

  Second Bar to the Distinguished Service Order.

    Lieut Col. L. Lloyd. D.S.O.

    The Military Cross.
  Captain H. Leeming.
  2/Lieutenant A. Searies.
  2/Lieutenant C.F. Mowatt.

  The Distinguished Conduct Medal.
  41987 Private W. Tingley.

    The Military Medal.
  53371 Sergt.(A/C.S.M.) G.A. Johnson.
  233054 Corporal   H.L. Cleaver.
  57584 Private   J. Hicklin.
  57465 "   E.A. Preston.
  63047 "   H. Brown.

War Diary

12th Suffolk Regt

December 1918

WAR DIARY

December 1918. 2^(nd) Suffolks.

Army Form C. 2118.

Place	Date	Hour	Summary of Events and Information	Remarks and references to Appendices
TOURCOING	Dec 1st to 31st		In billets. Training, Educational classes & recreation – etc.	

[Signature]
Lt Col
Comdg. 12th (S) (E.A.) Bn. Suffolk Regt.

12th Battalion The Suffolk Regiment.

	Officers.	Other Ranks.
Strength on 7th Dec. 1918.	43.	780.
Strength on 27th Dec. 1918.	45.	757.
Total reinforcements :-	2.	4.

Officers :— 2/Lieut. R.E. TATTERSALL.
2/Lieut. C.M. CAUTLEY.

Honours & Awards :-

Major A.M. CROSS.	M.C.	Croix de Guerre. (Division)
Private W. TINGLEY.	D.C.M.	" " " (Brigade)
" J. HICKEN.	M.M.	" " " "
Lieut Colonel L. LLOYD.	D.S.O.	MENTION.

Confidential

War Diary

12th Suffolk Regt

January 1919

Army Form C. 2118.

WAR DIARY
or
INTELLIGENCE SUMMARY.

(Erase heading not required.)

Instructions regarding War Diaries and Intelligence Summaries are contained in F. S. Regs., Part II. and the Staff Manual respectively. Title pages will be prepared in manuscript.

Place	Date	Hour	Summary of Events and Information	Remarks and references to Appendices
Jan 1st			The battalion moved by march route to B.U.6 in the Beuvres area, relieving the 18th Yorks & Lancs Regt.	
	Jan 4th to Jan 20th		Training and Education in Billeting area	
	Jan 21st		Presentation of arms to the Battalion at Roeux ? by Lieut. Genl. Sir Beauvoir de Lisle K.C.B, D.S.O	
	Jan 22nd to Jan 31st		Training and Education in Billeting area	

J Yates
Lieut & Ag Adj
1st Bn The Suffolk Regt.

Army Form C. 2118.

WAR DIARY
or
INTELLIGENCE SUMMARY.

February 1919. 12th Suffolk Regt. Vol 33

Place	Date	Hour	Summary of Events and Information	Remarks and references to Appendices
BONDUES	1st to 28th		Entitled. Demobilizing. Draft 6 officers and 199 ORs sent to 11th Suffolks for Army of occupation. W.	

Andrew
Capt. & Adjt.
12th Batt. Suffolk Regt.

12th Bn. The Suffolk Regiment.

	OFFICERS	OTHER RANKS
Strength on 1st February 1919	36	508
Strength on 28th February 1919	16	75

Honours during month:—

32471 Lance Corporal F. Simmons.   MILITARY MEDAL.

War Diary.

12th Bn Suffolk Regt.

March 1919

WAR DIARY
or
INTELLIGENCE SUMMARY.

Army Form C. 2118.

12th Bn. Suffolk Regt.   MARCH 1919

Place	Date	Hour	Summary of Events and Information	Remarks and references to Appendices
BONDUES Nr LILLE	1st to 31st		Reduced to Cadre Establishment - Cadre in civic to Bordeaux. Moveplan Stores taken to PETIT AUDENARDE dépôt interguera.	

R.N. Turner
Captain
12 Suffolks.

12th Bn. The Suffolk Regt.

	Officers	O.R.s
Strength 1st of Month.	16	75
" Last " "	9.	47.

Casualties   NIL.

Honours.

Captain F. ADAMS. awarded.
    CHEVALIER de L'ORDRE de LEOPOLD
            and.
    CROIX de - GUERRE.

WAR DIARY
or
INTELLIGENCE SUMMARY.

April 1919   12th Suffolk Regt.   Vol 35

Place	Date	Hour	Summary of Events and Information	Remarks and references to Appendices
BRUGES	April 1-2		At billets at cadre strength &c.	
HERSEAUX	3		Moved by march route & billets in HERSEAUX, Belgium &c.	
"	3-30		At billets at HERSEAUX as cadre awaiting to proceed to U.K. &c.	

[signature]
O.C. Cadre
12th Suffolk Regt.

12th Bn Suffolk Regt.

	Officers.	Other Ranks
Strength 1st of month.	7	50.
Strength last of month.	8.	105.

WAR DIARY 12th Bn Suffolk Regt.

MAY 1919

Place	Date	Hour	Summary of Events and Information	Remarks and references to Appendices
HERSEAUX (PETIT AUDENARDE)	1st to 31st		'Cadre' in billets awaiting return to England. nd.	

[signature]
Capt. & Adjt.
12th Batt. SUFFOLK REGT.

1st Bn. Suffolk Regt.

	OFFICERS.	OTHER RANKS.
Strength First of month.	8.	45.
Strength Last of month.	5.	37.

A. Arthur
CAPT. & ADJT.
12TH BATT. SUFFOLK REGT.

www.ingramcontent.com/pod-product-compliance
Lightning Source LLC
Chambersburg PA
CBHW081457160426
43193CB00013B/2519